# PEGASUS ENCYCLOPEDIA
# GOLF

Edited by: Pallabi B. Tomar, Hitesh Iplani
Managing editor: Tapasi De
Designed by: Vijesh Chahal, Nirbhay Kumar
Illustrated by: Suman S. Roy, Tanoy Choudhury
Colouring done by: Vinay Kumar, Kiran Kumari & Pradeep Kumar

# CONTENTS

What is golf? ..................................................... 3

Golf course ........................................................ 4

Equipments ...................................................... 11

The game ......................................................... 15

Par ..................................................................... 20

Scoring systems in golf .................................. 21

Other golf games ............................................ 23

Golf etiquette ................................................... 24

Golf tours and championships ..................... 25

Golf legends .................................................... 27

Test Your Memory .......................................... 31

Index ................................................................. 32

# What is golf?

Golf is an outdoor game and it is mostly played on specially constructed golf courses, each of which has a unique design. In golf, a player tries to put a small ball into various holes dug into the ground with the help of a club. The player who is able to cover all the holes in the least number of hits possible, is declared the winner of the game.

## Origin

A clear and certain evidence of the origin of the game is not available. However, it is popularly accepted that the game of golf as we know it today, originated in Scotland around the 15th century. The game was played by shepherds by knocking pebbles into rabbit holes on the present site of the Old Course at St Andrews. The first international golf match was held in 1682 between the Duke of York and George Patterson of Scotland on one side and two military noblemen of the English Army on the other.

### Astonishing fact

According to a popular legend, the word 'GOLF' stands for 'Gentlemen Only, Ladies Forbidden'!! However, this is not true. The word 'golf' comes from the Dutch word 'kolf' which means a stick, club or a bat.

# Golf course

Golf is played on specially constructed golf courses which stretch over a large area of land covered mostly with grass. A golf course consists of a series of holes. The area leading up to each hole is divided into various sections like a teeing area or a teeing ground, fairway, rough, hazards and a putting green with the pin (flagstick) and the cup. The grass is cut into different levels so as to increase difficulty or to aid in putting the ball into the hole. The standard number of holes in a golf course is 18. However, courses with nine holes are also common. On a nine-hole golf course the game is played twice.

### Astonishing fact

The Old Links, Musselburgh, near Edinburgh is the oldest playing golf course of the world.

## The teeing area

The 'teeing area', also known as the tee box, is the starting place for the hole for which the player is playing. It is a rectangular area whose length is equal to the length of two golf clubs.

The limits of the tee box in the front and on the sides are marked by the two tee-markers (coloured objects used to mark an area). The grass in this area is finely cropped and is on a lower level than the grass around it.

Sand (or a sand/seed mixture) is used to fill in any cavity left on the teeing surface after hitting.

It is important that the ball is well within the tee area while making the tee-shot. For the player however, it is not necessary to stand within the tee-box while making the shot.

> Originally, the teeing area had a mound of sand which was used by golfers as the modern tee to raise the ball over the surface.

# GOLF

The teeing area is called so because it is the only place in the whole golf course where the player might use a 'tee' to play his shot. A tee is a nail like support for raising the ball above the ground.

Usually, blue markers indicate the longest distance to the hole and are meant for players with a low handicap. White markers are used to indicate a shorter distance and are meant for men with a middle handicap. Red markers indicate a tee box with the shortest distance to the hole, and is known as the ladies' tee or the senior's tee.

Tee markers are moved around often so as to save the teeing ground from severe damage in any one spot. Tee markers can be varied in shape and size as well as material. The number of tee blocks and the colors used are decided by each club.

**Nicklaus North golf course in British Colombia, Canada has markers shaped like a bear!!**

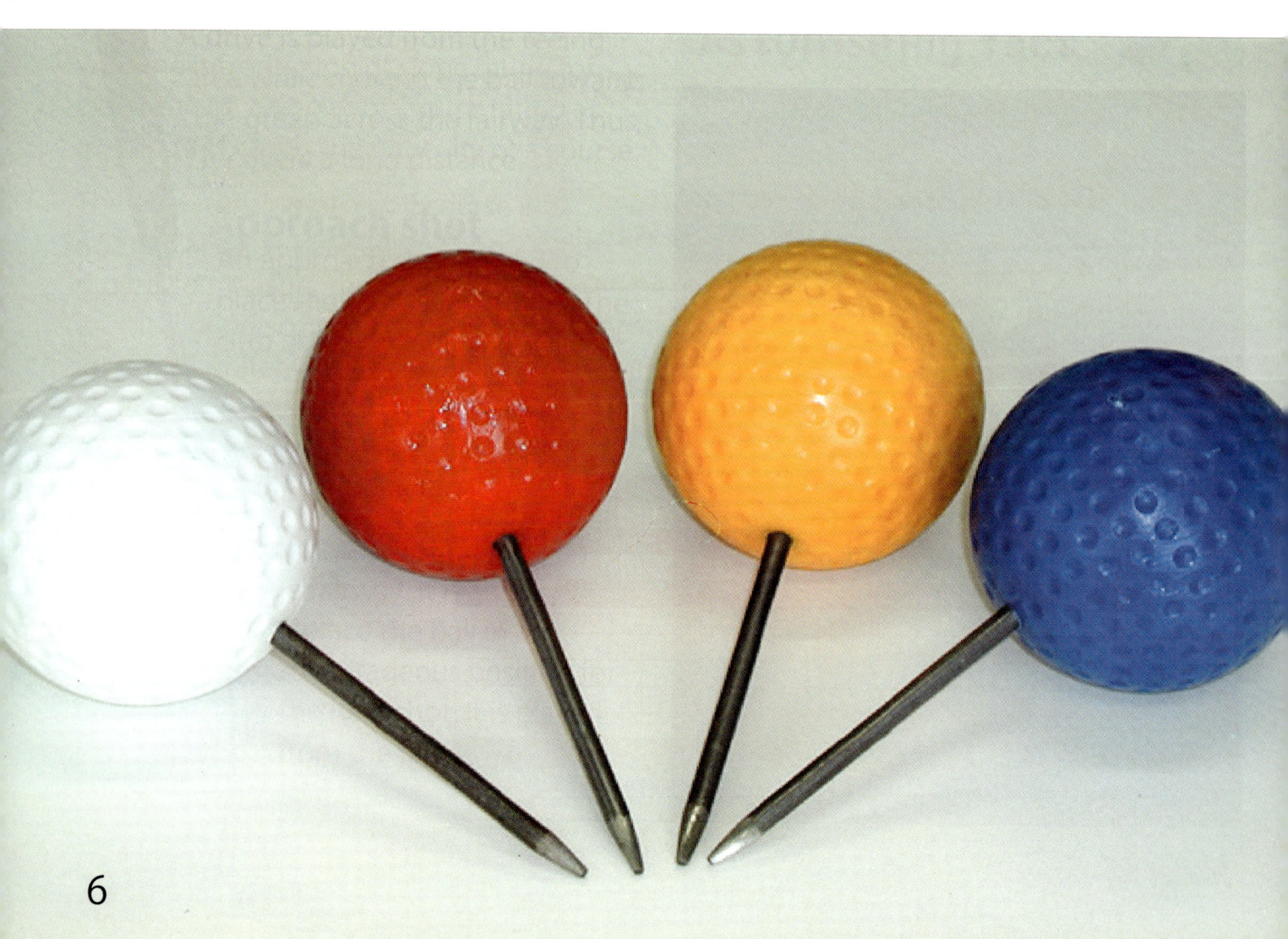

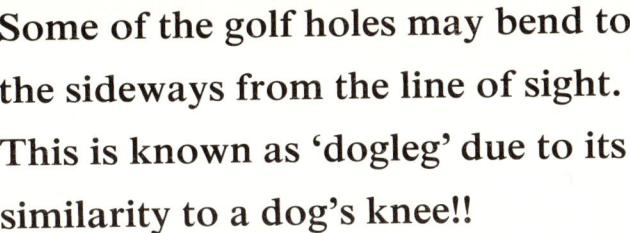

Golf course

## Fairway and rough

Once the tee shot has been played, the player tries to hit the ball again towards the putting green from the spot at which it stopped. In between the teeing area and the putting green, lie the fairway and the rough. in some cases, to reach the putting green the player must make an extra shot from the fairway or the rough depending on where his ball lands.

The fairway is a closely mowed part of the golf course that runs from the teeing area to the putting green. It is a favourable area for the player to hit a shot.

Rough is the area between the fairway and the green. The grass here is cut higher than that of the fairway. The rough is not a favourable area for the player.

The roll of the ball is influenced by the quality of the grass. It also affects the ability of the player to control the ball. Height of the grass and the quality of the mowing also influences the play of the course.

### Astonishing fact

Some of the golf holes may bend to the sideways from the line of sight. This is known as 'dogleg' due to its similarity to a dog's knee!!

## Ground under repair (GUR)

Ground under repair is an area which is damaged or is under repair. It is usually indicated by a white line drawn around it. A player should not play from this area. If his ball drops into GUR a player can lift it up and can resume play from the nearest good spot.

## Hazards

Hazards are natural or man-made obstructions in the golf course which are used to make a game more challenging and interesting.

Types of hazard:

(a) Water hazards

(b) Man-made hazards (bunkers or sand traps)

**Water hazards** are areas of water on the golf course that either cut across the hole being played or lie alongside it. The player should try to hit the ball over the water hazard.

### Astonishing fact

Jason Zuback of Canada who holds the record for the fastest ever golf drive at 204 miles per hour! He is also a five-time World Long Drive Champion.

Golf course

A **bunker** is a man-made depression on the ground of the golf course in which the soil has been replaced with sand. Bunkers do not have fixed size and shape. Bunkers are usually placed on the either side of the fairway, in the middle of the fairway or in spots around the putting green.

Balls that fall in a hazard are to be played under special rules. A player is not allowed to touch the ground with his club before playing a ball. A ball lying in a hazard must be played from the same spot.

However, if the ball cannot be played from the hazard the player is allowed to hit the ball from some other spot. A penalty of one stroke is charged from the player under such conditions.

## Astonishing fact

About 25 percent of the golfers in the world are women.

## Putting green

Putting green is the area where the hole is located. The grass in the area of the putting green is very finely cut so that the ball can roll long distances.

In this area, the player tries to roll the ball towards the hole and finally into the cup. A stroke played on the putting green is known as a putt. The ball should never be lifted in the air once inside the putting green.

The cup is a metal container inside the hole. It has a diameter of 4.25 inches and a depth of at least 3.94 inches. The cup has a flag on a pole stationed in it usually called pin or a flagstick. It is used so that the location of the hole is visible from a distance.

# Equipments

## Golf ball

A golf ball is a small white coloured ball with a hard rubber core, with a minimum diameter of 1.680 inches. Its weight should not exceed the specified limit of 45.93 grams.

First golf balls were made out of wood. Later on they were made out of leather casing stuffed with feathers.

The surface usually has a pattern of 300-400 dimples designed to improve the ball's ability to move in air or on the ground.

## Golf clubs

A player carries several clubs during the game. The maximum number of clubs a player can carry according to the rules of the game is fourteen.

Players use three major kinds of golf clubs— woods, irons and putters.

> **Golf balls do not have the same number of dimples. The ideal ball will usually have between 380 and 432 dimples.**

# GOLF

Woods are used for long shots from the tee or fairway. Irons are used for precision shots from fairways as well as from the rough. Wedges are irons used to play shorter shots.

A 'hybrid' club is often used for long shots from difficult rough. Putters are mostly used on the green to roll the ball into the hole.

Clubhead covers are used to protect the clubs from the damage caused due to striking each other, and from weather and incidental damages while in the bag.

### Astonishing fact

On an Apollo 14 mission in 1971, astronaut Alan B. Shepard played golf on the moon!! As a result, there are two golf balls somewhere on the moon or in the space!!

## The tee

The tee is a nail like object with a small resting place for the ball on its head. They are made of plastic or wood. Tees are used to lift the ball above the ground so as to make the stroke easier. Tees can only be used while making the first shot from the tee-box

# Equipments

## Golf bag

A golf bag is used to move golf clubs around the golf course as he plays. Golf bags also have various pockets for carrying equipment and supplies required during the game.

Golf bags have both a hand strap and shoulder strap for carrying, and sometimes have retractable legs that allow the bag to stand upright when at rest.

## Golf cart

Golf carts are motorized vehicles used by the players to move around the golf course and carry their equipment.

### Astonishing fact

International Golf Club in Massachusetts which measures 9104.22 m is the longest golf course in the world!!

# GOLF

## Players' clothing

Golf is usually played with one player only.

Golfers normally wear comfortable polo shirts with trousers. Some golf clubs have a defined dress code.

## Gloves

Golfers wear gloves that help them grip the club properly and prevent blistering. Usually, a glove is worn on the non-dominant hand only.

## Shoes

Special shoes with metal or plastic spikes attached to the soles are worn by golfers to increase traction and thus helping them maintain balance on a wet ground.

# The game

A round of golf is played by covering a series of holes in a given order. A series usually consists of 18 holes that are played in the order dictated by the layout of the golf course. On a nine-hole course, the game is completed by playing 2 rounds. Play starts with the first stroke in the teeing area. The golfer may use a tee for the first shot if he desires to. Tee is generally used while making a long shot.

Players are sometimes accompanied by a **caddy**, who carry and manage the players' equipment and who sometimes give advice on the choice of the clubs and the kind of shot to be played.

> The word caddy comes from the French word 'cadpets' which in medieval France meant the not so worthy sons of a noble family. In English the term became 'caddie' and came to mean any useless kid on the street who could be hired for the day to carry around golf clubs!!

# GOLF

## Penalties

A golf player who covers the golf course in the minimum number of strokes, is considered to be a winner. Penalties are charged on players by adding extra strokes to their score as a punishment. Penalty strokes are also added for disobeying of rules or for hitting one's ball in a spot where it cannot be played.

A lost ball or a ball hit out of bounds can cause a penalty of one stroke and extra distance. Hitting a wrong ball or putting a fellow golfer's ball incurs a two stroke penalty. Rule infractions can also lead to disqualification.

### Astonishing fact

At the golf course on the island of Tonga near New Zealand there's no penalty if a monkey steals your golf ball!!

# The game

## Types of shots

Golfers play different kinds of shots according to the location of the ball on the golf course. The first step of playing a golf stroke is the pre-stroke which means choosing the club and the position. Various strokes employed by golfers are:

## Normal shot

Till the time the green (or fairway) is reached, golfers use a normal swing to hit the ball. It consists of a 'backward swing', a 'forward swing' back to the middle (where the ball is hit), and a 'follow-through'.

Clubs which are used while playing this stroke are woods or irons.

## Pitch shot

In a pitch shot the ball lands mostly on the greens and does not move much after that.

## Flop shot

In a flop shot a lofted wedge is used. As a result of the hit, the ball rises at a very high angle, and then lands softly on the ground followed by a soft roll. The shot is used for small distances usually while overcoming a hazard.

### Astonishing fact

In 1912, after her tee shot fell into the river, Maud McInnes climbed in a boat and attempted to play and bring the ball which was floating away, on dry land. She finally succeeded after a mile and a half and 166 strokes!!

## Chip shot

In a chip shot the ball lands on the ground softly and then rolls down towards the hole. This shot is used within a short range around the green. Chippers, or a short iron or wedge is mostly used to play this shot.

## Putt shot

The putt shot putts the ball in the hole or brings it closer to the hole from the green. The club used is called putter. The club moves straight back and swings through gently along the same path.

A drive is played from the teeing area while moving the ball towards the green across the fairway. Thus, it covers a long distance.

## Approach shot

An approach shot is used to place the ball on the green. The club used is a short-range iron.

## Lay-up shot

A lay-up shot is a highly accurate shot employed to avoid a hazard lying on the fairway. It is also used to place the ball in an advantageous position for the next shot. It is played from the fairway after the drive and travels a short distance.

## Pitch shot

A pitch shot travels a little more distance than the chip shot requiring a slightly stronger swing. A lofted club is used for playing this shot and the ball stops very quickly once it reaches the green.

## Bunker shot

A shot played from a sand trap is known as a bunker shot. A lofted wedge is used to play the shot. The shot carries the ball high so as to take it beyond the bunker and land it safely within the greens.

## Astonishing fact

The longest drive ever (563 m) was made by Mike Austin during the US National Seniors Open Championship on Sept. 25, 1974!!

## Bunker shot

A shot played from a sand trap is known as a bunker shot. A lofted wedge is a kind of club which is used to play the shot. The shot carries the ball high so as to take it beyond the bunker and land it safely within the greens.

## Draw shot

In a draw, the ball moves from the right to the left during flight. The ball will move from left to right for a left-handed player.

## Whiff or an air-shot

A whiff or an air-shot is when the golfer completely misses the ball.

## Slice shot

A slice shot occurs when the ball flies severely from left to right or vice versa for a left-handed player.

## Hook shot

A hook occurs when the ball flies severely from right to left or vice versa for a left-handed player.

## Astonishing fact

There are about 50 million golfers in the world!!

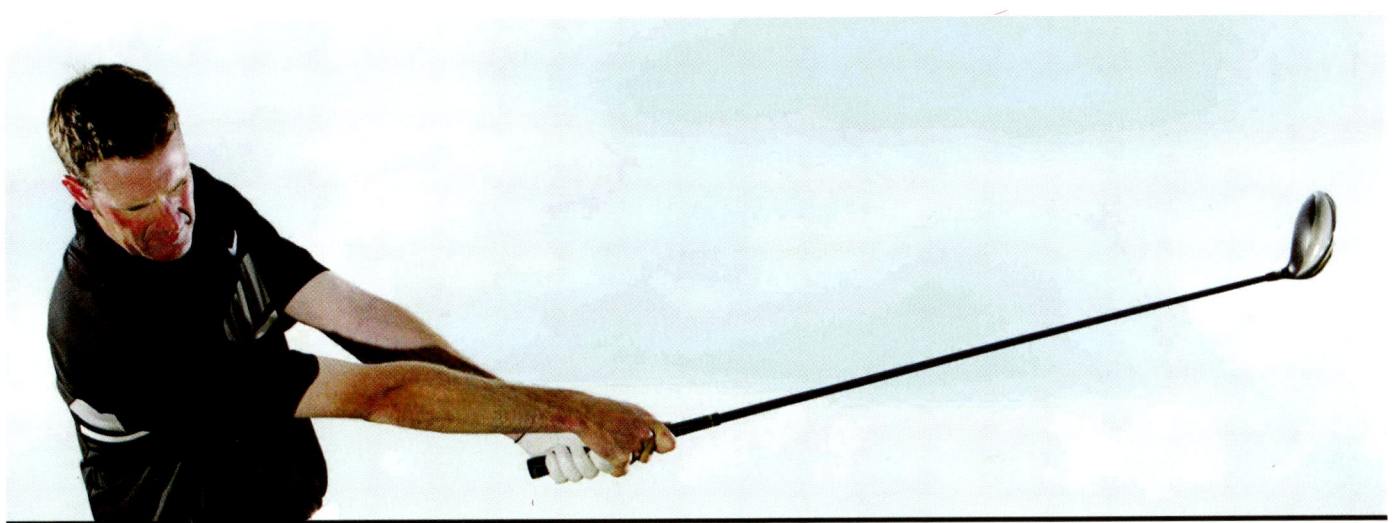

# Par

Par it means the expected number of strokes an expert player needs to cover a single hole on the course. It is one of the most prevalent scorecard systems in golf.

The par of a hole is divided on the basis of the distance from the tee to the green. Normally a par-three hole is less than 225 m in length, a par-four hole is in the range of 225–434 m, and a par-five hole is more than 435 m. Par-six and par-seven holes are uncommon but do exist. They can be more than 595 m in length.

### Astonishing fact

Tiger Woods was introduced to golf at the age of nine months by his father.

The term 'par' derives from the stock exchange term 'par' that means a stock maybe above or below its normal or 'par' figure!!

# Scoring systems in golf

Golf competitions use different kinds of scoring systems. These are:

**Matchplay:** In this type of a game, each time a player is successful in putting the ball into a hole, it is considered to be a match. If both players have equal score the game is tied.

**Strokeplay:** It is the simplest method of scoring. Each player adds up his score, and after deducting the handicaps the player with the lowest score wins.

**Stableford:** Stableford is the most common of all the used scoring systems. In this system the player adds his full handicap to the points scored to get his total points at the end of the round.

The goal in any type of golf match is to complete a round in the minimum number of strokes possible. Different terms are used to describe the scores of a golfer in reference to the par of a hole and the number of shots he made.

If, for e.g., the par for a hole is five (that is, a skilled golfer needs to make at least five shots to finish a hole) and a player finishes that hole in four shots then it is called a 'Birdie'. In other words, the golfer has taken 1 shot less than the expected par.

Similarly, if a golfer takes more shots (it maybe 1, 2, 3 or more shots) than the expected par, then also the scores have specific names.

Given below is a table explaining this:

| In Numbers | Term | Description |
| --- | --- | --- |
| −5 | Ostrich | 5 shots below par |
| −4 | Condor | 4 shots below par |
| −3 | Albatross | 3 shots below par |
| −2 | Eagle | 2 shots below par |
| −1 | Birdie | 1 shot below par |
| E | Par | equal to par |
| +1 | Bogey | 1 shot above par |
| +2 | Double Bogey | 2 shots above par |
| +3 | Triple Bogey | 3 shots above par |
| +4 | Quadruple Bogey | 4 shots above par |

**When a golfer manages to sink his ball into the cup in a single drive from the tee, then it is known as an ace (or a hole in one).**

# GOLF

## Golf handicap

The handicap system in golf enables players of varying golfing abilities to compete with each other equally. Each golfer is awarded a handicap rating based on his performance. Other sports also have a handicap system, but it works most effectively in the game of golf only.

Handicap means the number of extra strokes a player receives for a hole. Higher handicap means more extra strokes received. The highest official handicaps are 28 for men and 45 for women. An expert golfer plays from 'scratch' or zero handicap or even a 'plus' handicap. The handicap system was restructured in the early 1980s with the introduction of slope rating for golf courses, along with course rating as methods of rating the difficulty of a course.

The course rating of a golf course is a numerical value between 67 and 77 that is used to measure the average good score by an expert golfer with a handicap of zero (scratch handicap) on that course.

The slope rating of a golf course is a number between 55 and 155 that defines the difficulty of a course for a golfer with a handicap of 18 or more.

Par plays no role in computing handicaps.

## The golf scorecard

Golf courses have their own specific scorecards. The card shows information regarding the club, like an outline map of the course layout, and the colours of the flags on the different holes, the local rules of that club, the number of holes, and the length for each of the tee types. The totals are summarized at the bottom of the card and the net score is written in a large box.

The card is then signed by both the players and the score marker (a person who keeps the score) and the failure to do so results in disqualification.

### Astonishing fact

80% of all the golfers of the world will never have a handicap rating below 18!!

| HOLE | 1 | 2 | 3 | 4 | 5 | 6 | 7 | 8 | 9 | OUT |
|---|---|---|---|---|---|---|---|---|---|---|
| BACK TEES 68.6/114 | 253 | 400 | 152 | 395 | 322 | 168 | 375 | 345 | 495 | 2905 |
| SENIOR TEES 63.9/110 | 223 | 360 | 132 | 340 | 284 | 105 | 324 | 281 | 443 | 2492 |
| PAR | 4 | 4 | 3 | 4 | 4 | 3 | 4 | 4 | 5 | 35 |
| HANDICAP | 17 | 1 | 15 | 5 | 13 | 11 | 3 | 7 | 9 | |
| | | | | | | | | | | |
| | | | | | | | | | | |
| | | | | | | | | | | |
| | | | | | | | | | | |
| HANDICAP | 7 | 1 | 17 | 11 | 13 | 15 | 9 | 5 | 3 | |
| LADIES TEES 68.9/107 | 223 | 359 | 96 | 290 | 286 | 105 | 324 | 281 | 406 | 2370 |
| YELLOW TEES | • | • | • | • | • | • | • | • | • | |

# Other golf games

## Skins

In a skins game, each hole is treated as a separate contest. Skin is the term used for the prize money assigned to each hole. The game is usually played for prize money on the professional level or as a means of a bet for amateurs. Skin carries over to next hole if the hole is tied (or halved). If you come to the end of the round and there are still skins left over, play continues until the final skin has been decided.

The following golf games are played in a team play:

## Foursome

A foursome is played between two teams of two players each, in which each team has only one ball and players take turns playing it.

## Four-ball

A four-ball is also played between two teams of two players each, but every player plays his/her own ball and for each team the lower score on each hole is counted.

## Scramble

In scramble, each player plays a tee shot from the tee. Then the best tee shot from the shots played is selected. Players of the team then play their second shot from within a club length of the location of the best shot. This is repeated until the hole is completed. In a champagne scramble, each player in team plays a tee shot on each hole. The location of the ball from the best shot is used and all players play their own ball from this spot. In best ball, each player plays each hole as normal, but the lowest score of all the players on the team counts as the team's score. This game is also known as Ambrose or Best shot.

## Greensome

In a greensome, also called modified alternate shot, two players tee off, and then pick the location of the ball from the best shot as in a scramble. The player with the best first shot allows the other player to play the second shot. The play then alternates as in a foursome.

A type of greensome is also played at times in which the opposing team chooses which of their opponent's tee shots their opponents should use. The player who did not shoot the chosen first shot plays the second shot. Play then continues as a greensome.

## Shotgun

A shotgun is a sort of start of a tournament match in which different groups of players start on different holes. This allows for all players to start and end their round at the same time.

# Golf etiquette

The etiquettes of golf refer to the code of conduct that the golfers around the world must follow whether playing in a competition or casually. The etiquettes of golf make sure that every player can play the game of golf under safe conditions.

These codes are set by golf clubs and do not differ greatly from club to club.

Some of the golf etiquettes are:

- One should not move, converse or stand close to or behind the ball or the hole when a player is making a swing or stroke as it can not only be dangerous but it can also affect the focus of the player adversely
- A player should hit only after making it sure that the players in the front are out of range
- Players should immediately leave the putting green once they are done. Cards must be marked before starting from the next tee
- The player who has the honour, that is whose score is the lowest, shall be allowed to play before his opponent or fellow competitor tees the ball
- When a shot from the bunker is played, a player should fill up all the holes made by him during the play. He should leave the rake in the direction of the play
- A player should ensure that any cut left by his stroke on the green is filled up and repaired
- A golfer should be careful, patient and pleasant to those not so competent in the game
- The players should try to keep their carts off the grass as much as possible
- The players should respect the pace of the game and should not hold up the game too much. One should not spend too much time looking for a lost ball

# Golf tours and championships

Golf tours are organized by professional golf associations (PGA) or by independent tour organizations. There are at least twenty professional golf tours.

Each tour has members who participate in most of its event. At times non-members are also invited to compete in some of them. In order to be a part of an elite tour, a player needs to be highly competent. There are six major tours for women, each based in a different country or continent. The most esteemed tour for women is the United States based LPGA Tour.

The most popular tour is the PGA Tour. This is because most PGA Tour events have a prize money of at least US $800,000. The PGA European Tour ranks second to the PGA Tour.

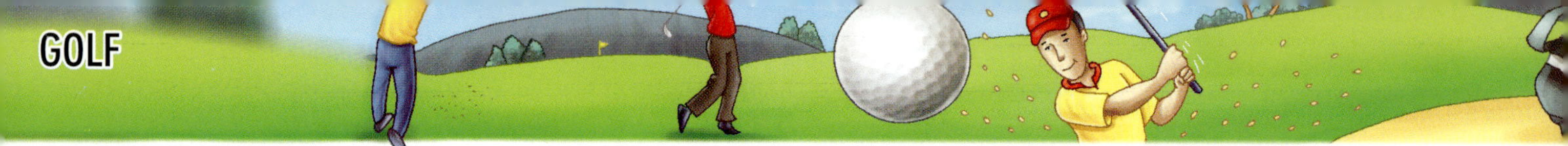

## Major championships

The four major men's championships in chronological order are: The Masters, the U.S. Open, The Open Championship (also called the British Open) and the PGA Championship.

These events attract the top golfers from all over the world.

## Major golf tours

The PGA European Tour also attracts a good number of top golfers from outside North America and is next to the PGA Tour in worldwide importance. The other leading men's tours are the Japan Golf Tour, the Asian Tour, the PGA Tour of Australasia, and the Sunshine Tour.

Many senior tours for men of 50 and above also take place. The most prestigious seniors golf tour is the U.S. based Champions Tour.

### Astonishing fact

Woods is the only player to have won all four professional major championships in a row!

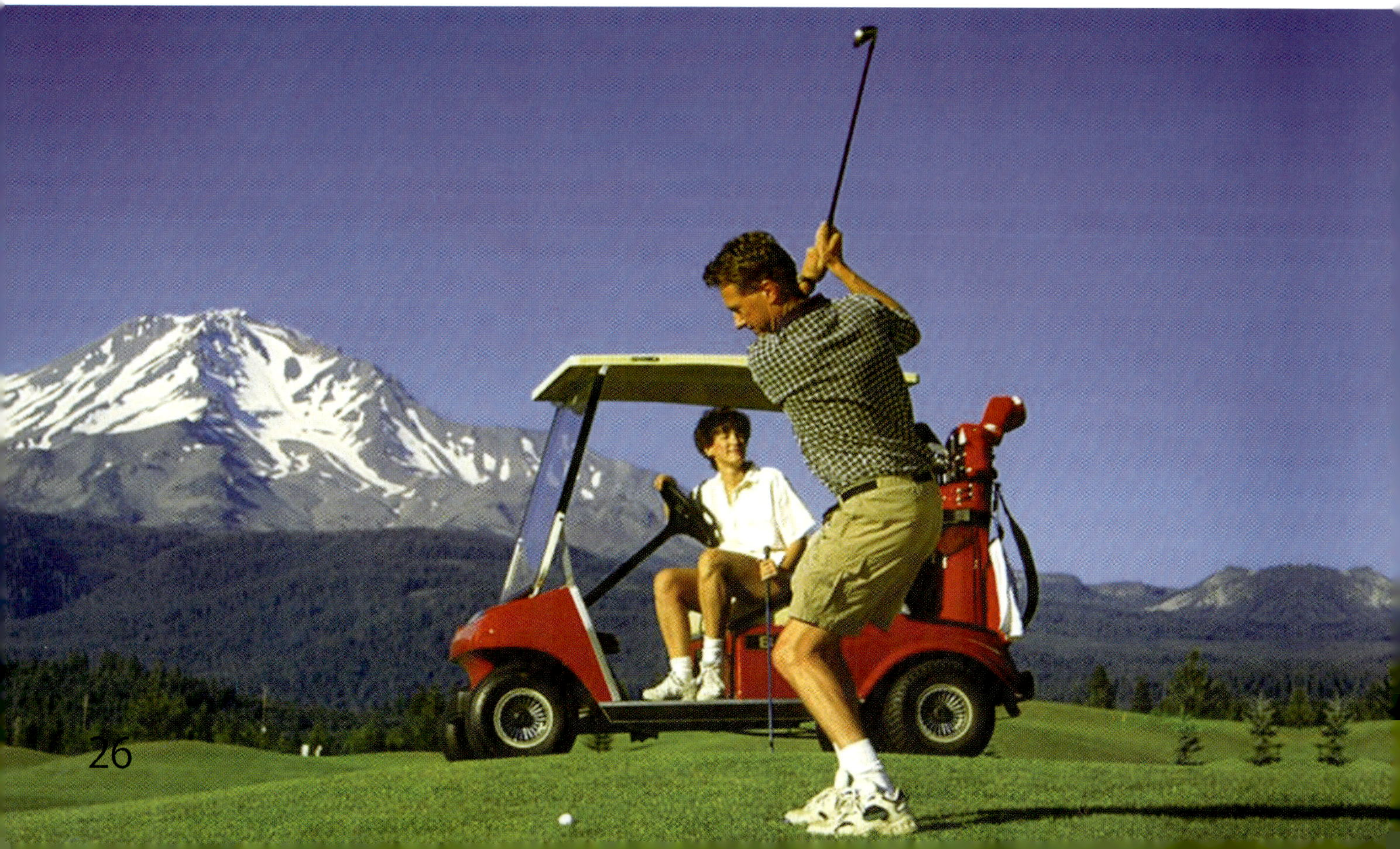

# Golf legends

| | |
|---|---|
| **Name:** | Tiger Woods |
| **Nickname:** | Tiger |
| **Country:** | United States of America |
| **Majors:** | 14 |
| **Professional wins:** | 97 |
| **Achievements:** | Woods has won 71 official PGA Tour events including 14 majors. He has the lowest career scoring average and the most career earnings in PGA Tour history. |

> **Woods is the youngest player ever to complete the grand slam - winning all four of golf's majors by the age of 20.**

| | |
|---|---|
| **Name:** | Greg Norman |
| **Nickname:** | The great white shark |
| **Country:** | Australia |
| **Majors:** | 2 |
| **Professional wins:** | 88 |
| **Achievements:** | He has won the Arnold Palmer Award for being the leading money winner three times on the US PGA tour (1986, 89, and 95). He was also the first person in the history of the Tour to cross $10 millions in career earnings. Norman was inducted into the World Golf Hall of Fame in 2001. |

# GOLF

| | |
|---|---|
| Name: | Nick Faldo |
| Nickname: | ----- |
| Country: | England |
| Majors: | 6 |
| Professional wins: | 40 |
| Achievements: | Faldo was selected as the BBC Sports Personality of the Year in 1989 and was inducted into the World Golf Hall of Fame in 1997. In 2000, Faldo was placed as the 18th greatest golfer of all time by Golf Digest magazine. He was knighted in 2009 Birthday Honours for his services to golf. |

| | |
|---|---|
| Name: | Severiano Ballesteros |
| Nickname: | Seve |
| Country: | Spain |
| Majors: | 5 |
| Professional wins: | 91 |
| Achievements: | In 2000, Ballesteros was selected as the 16th greatest golfer of all time by Golf Digest magazine. In 1999, Ballesteros was inducted into the World Golf Hall of Fame. |

| | |
|---|---|
| Name: | Ian Woosnam |
| Nickname: | Woosie |
| Country: | Wales |
| Majors: | 1 |
| Professional wins: | 47 |
| Achievements: | He has won the prestigious BBC Wales Sports Personality of the Year award three times. He was awarded an O.B.E. in the 2007. |

# Golf legends

| | |
|---|---|
| **Name:** | Nick Price |
| **Nickname:** | ----- |
| **Country:** | Zimbabwe |
| **Majors:** | 3 |
| **Professional wins:** | 48 |
| **Achievements:** | One of the best players in the world, Nick has topped the PGA Tour money list two times. He has spent 43 weeks at number one in the Official World Golf Rankings. Price was inducted into the World Golf Hall of Fame in 2003. |

| | |
|---|---|
| **Name:** | Vijay Singh |
| **Nickname:** | The Big Fijian |
| **Country:** | Fiji |
| **Majors:** | 3 |
| **Professional wins:** | 58 |
| **Achievements:** | He has the most number of wins as a non-American player (34) on the PGA Tour. He is on the 14th rank on the all-time list. He was inducted into the World Golf Hall of Fame in 2006. He is the youngest living person to have entered the World Golf Hall of Fame. |

| | |
|---|---|
| **Name:** | Fred Couples |
| **Nickname:** | Mr Skins, Boom Boom |
| **Country:** | United States of America |
| **Professional wins:** | 50 |
| **Majors:** | 1 |
| **Achievements:** | He has a total of 15 PGA tour wins, including The Players Championship twice and one major win, The Masters Tournament in 1992. Couples has been named the PGA Tour Player of the Year twice. |

# GOLF

| | |
|---|---|
| **Name:** | Ernie Els |
| **Nickname:** | The big easy |
| **Country:** | SA |
| **Majors:** | 3 |
| **Professional wins:** | 62 |
| **Achievements:** | He won the World Match Play Championship seven times, a record in its own. He also won three major championships: the U.S. Open in 1994 and 1997 and The Open Championship in 2002. |

| | |
|---|---|
| **Name:** | Bernhard Langer |
| **Nickname:** | ----- |
| **Country:** | Germany |
| **Majors:** | 2 |
| **Professional wins:** | 83 |
| **Achievements:** | He has won the Masters championship two times. Also he was the inaugural World Number 1 when the Official World Golf Rankings were introduced in 1986. He was inducted into the World Golf Hall of Fame in 2001. He was also appointed as an honorary OBE. |

| | |
|---|---|
| **Name:** | Jack Nicklaus |
| **Nickname:** | The golden bear |
| **Country:** | United States of America |
| **Majors:** | 18 |
| **Professional wins:** | 115 |
| **Achievements:** | He has received the PGA Tour Player of the Year five times. He has topped the PGA Tour money list eight times. Nicklaus was inducted into the World Golf Hall of Fame in 1974 and the Canadian Golf Hall of Fame in 1995. |

# Test Your MEMORY

1. Where did golf originate?
2. When was the first international golf match held?
3. Which is the oldest golf course in the world?
4. What is the minimum allowed diametre of a golf cup?
5. What is the diametre of a golf ball?
6. What is the maximum number of golf clubs a player can carry on the field at all times during the game?
7. What are the two types of hazards on a golf course?
8. What is the number of dimples on a golf ball?
9. How many holes are there in a standard golf course?
10. What are the highest official handicaps for men and women?
11. Name the four major men's championships in golf.
12. What are the three types of scoring systems in golf?

# Index

## A
air shot 9
approach shot 8

## B
bunker 8 9 8 9 24
bunker shot 8 9

## C
caddy 5
chip shot 8
clubs 5 2 3 4
 5 7 24
cup 4 2

## D
draw 9
drive 8 9 2

## F
fairway 4 7 9 2 7
 8
flop shot 7
four ball 23
foursome 23

## G
gloves 4
golf bag 3
golf carts 3
golf courses 3 4 6 7 8
 9 3 5 6 7 22
greensome 23

## H
handicap 6 2 22
hazards 4 8
hole 3 4 5 6 7 8 9
 2 5 8 2
 2 22 23 24
hook 9

## I
irons 2

## L
lay up 8

## P
penalties 6
pitch shot 7 8
putt 8
putting green 4 7 9
 24
putt shot 8

## R
rough 4 7 2

## S
scorecard 2 22
scramble 23
shotgun 23
skins 23 29
slice 9

## T
teeing area 4 5 6 7 5
 8
the pin 4

## W
whiff 9
woods 2 7 26